THE WAY OF BEAUTY

THE WAY OF BEAUTY

BOOK OF LOVE

Oshun Seyi

Waterside Productions

Cover Design by Ana Soulful at www.marhstudios.com

First Printing, 2023

ISBN-13: 978-1-960583-37-6 print edition
ISBN-13: 978-1-960583-38-3 e-book edition

Waterside Productions

2055 Oxford Ave
Cardiff, CA 92007
www.waterside.com

TABLE OF CONTENTS

THE WAY OF BEAUTY

BOOK 1

INTRODUCTION & DEDICATION

'The Way of Beauty' is an offering of the fire and water, the divine eternal flame that resides in all and the flesh that is mainly water.

The spirit and the matter, the male and female, the formless and the form it is the connection of them both to reach the middle path of a peace- filled existence on earth.

My reason for this book is to be a humble messenger that there are other ways to heal. I am not an advocate for my way is the cure to all but to simply share my experiences on my own journey.

I dedicate all that I write about or that came through my being first and foremost to the magnificence of the spirit eternal ... the grace ... the creator of the unknown great mystery.

The essence of the writings —unconditional love.

A documentation of my experiences of coming back to the essence within; that is true love, absolute stillness, constant calm,non wavering warmth, glow of the heart ,being in mystery of the inviolable silence within that is the true nature of life.

I was given an invitation from the divine at the tender age of 6 when I was faced with 10 minutes to live in my mortal form everything in a moment disappeared. There was no form and as I fell into what I saw as stars in the universe something pulled me back my ego out of the fear of that unknown place which ever since I have been learning from as I realise now it was the fear of death. Before this experience I could see everything as fluid as energy in the ether when my head my ego took hold the real journey of surrender started.

As I had always feared death as a child this was obviously my mission to get over it!

Years passed and many near death experiences followed; remedies, teacher's, travels, lovers that all taught me earth lessons on the way. I can finally say I am not afraid of death as it does not exist. I am truly 100% with life in whatever form that takes .It's all a changing of form, that's all. The passage FROM THE BODY TO ANOTHER FORM IS SO FEARED YET IT IS HOW WE ALL GOT TO FORM FROM THE DARKNESS OF THE SPIRIT IN THE WOMB FROM THE ORIGINAL FORMLESS REALM INTO FORM THEN WE JUST MOVE FROM ONE CYCLE TO THE NEXT THERE IS NO FEAR REQUIRED IT S JUST INNERSTANDING THAT IS NEEDED FOR OUR HUMAN BEING TO REALISE IT IS JUST THAT BEING IN A SHELL OF A FORM THE BODY which is magnificent in itself but transient so why not just look after it and enjoy being in it until you have to vacate and become something else.

I am eternal life in whatever form that may take.

Just love, just be!!

I was told once by a great mother elder that we are here on earth to learn that's it - -self-refinement and that the question of life and death was never a priority, as ancient beings knew that and so could spend time on other great pursuits.

How strange that in the west our ways seem to be focussed on possessions and youth, all of which cannot be taken with us after the body has died .Instead of spending the whole of our lives worried about losing things, why not use the time wisely to explore and investigate who we are, beautiful bodies expressing our oneness individually through the way of the heart-the way of beauty.

I had a huge aversion to being told what to do at the age of 8. I would roller skate outside around where my Granny and Grampy lived until really late.

My Granny would have to chase me and shout for ages for me to come in, I thought she was being mean, obviously now I realise it was for my own safety and that it was dark and time for dinner and bed.

I used to get so mad with my sister and Granny. They were so good, pure and disciplined whilst I was free and wild!!

Today both are now with our ancestors and I realise this discipline they had was actually freedom.

Being wild and exploring is a great adventure but I think incorporating discipline along this life journey is the ultimate tool leading to a discovered new freedom.

There is natural law on this planet and in the stars and beyond all the multi universes of the cosmos and it is ok to follow it. I found out in fact it is imperative we do.

Surrendering to the magic and order of the universe is paramount for human existence but I am just starting to realise it is not great science. It's actually within our own compass magnet of our hearts that can lead us to the intuition of the directions we all individually and as a collective require.

There is a manual inside each of us and clarity comes and will come to all of us if we can just listen!!

I know when I do not surrender my life falls apart so I now listen and follow the map of my heart.

WHY I WROTE THE BOOK.

An offering of my personal journey of healing the mind, the body and the soul to unite with the divine.

I wrote this book during the last 5 years whilst I was finishing my physical healing from my body being full of tumours.

Although it is still a daily mission to keep healthy, the experiences that aid me and the guidance of pain and pleasure I went through, since I delved into the darkness to emerge into the light that I started in 2007 are what I wanted to share.

We as humans are not alone and if anyone is suffering like I was I would be so blessed and grateful if my words and information could help them.

None of our journeys are the same on this our Grandmother the earth but sharing wisdom and knowledge is vital for our healing at this time.

Mitakuye Oyas'in

'We are all one we are all related' Lakotah nation proverb.

The beginning ... the real hard work!!

'Can you follow an ant?'

The Elder asks ...

'Yes of course'

I reply

'Ok then can you follow a snail?'

The Elder asks

'Yes I can'

I say

The Elder smiles ...

Little did I know when I thought I had done my healing from 2007-2010 that I had not even begun!

This is when I really met my shadow ...

GLIMPSE *

Into the twinkle of the stars ...
To discover that which does not come from ease
Is that which will host a myriad of changes.
Just as the prisms of light enfold each of us within and without.

Do not run from the shadows that you hold, only integrate them within your own self and laugh at the way they sometimes cast over your spirit like transient clouds. The shadow self is there not to hide away in but to go deeper into so that the light can emerge.

Only day arises from night-if night was not dark we could not see the stars!

The beauty of the night and the beauty of the day-same same.

Love exists beyond light and shade in the formless void. This is the way ... the way of beauty.

GUIDANCE 1

Graced with light your heart is vibrant,
  Unknowing yet pure and silent … this stillness can move mountains.

  In that paradox that has such depth only inside knowing can know,
  Without this everything seems relentless and pushing.

  Flow like the water of life for this is the formless freedom of the sea,
  All creatures great and small that roam this land and think they have to
fall.
  This is not the case, searching for inside grace is the key.
  So be who you are, dance and love unconditionally.

GUIDANCE 2

True love just is a vibration of steadiness. Passion and desire are part of the divine too, as long as there is purity of spirit with it. Keeping in balance, reason needs no discovery when the heart is bathed in the fires of purity.

Love holds no one in control, nor does it let you go with no holding; for true love is eternally safe and warm. As the heart beats inside the mother's body the infant hears the primal call and it is known that the unknown is all around. Inside the womb it is dark, we are blind and in water, but we are pure in creation and being created. How strange that once released into the light, we are then afraid of the dark, of the unknown of creation, from which we came.

Practical's- Words of Inspiration to Rest With

Recreation

Peace

Love

Happiness

Reflections of Light

Understanding

Honour and Respect

Patience

Compassion

Non-Judgemental Behaviour

Acceptance

Honesty

Genuineness

Integrity

Reason

Truth

Essence

GUIDANCE 3

<u>Guidance of the Male and Female Energies in Action in Physicality</u>

Observations of each and the other's form at all times is essential. A woman is a lover; a sister; and mother to her chosen mate a man is a lover; a brother; and a father to his chosen mate. These dynamics are integral in all love-based intimate relationships. When a man is seeing his mate as a sister and she is seeing him as a father, in that moment a certain emotion is perpetrated within the couple. Usually, this is when discomfort arises. It is something like elements being out of balance. If Earth is moist, and Fire is tame, it will not spread and burn, it will gently go to the form of embers: soft and warm. Thus, Fire and Earth are united in harmony. As is with Water and Air, if Air is in turmoil, as with a hurricane, then Water is also in turmoil both fight against each other, thus ending in destruction. When a gentle breeze rests on a serene sea, both elements calm and ease each other. These elements of Air, Fire, Water, Earth and Ether are within us and like the archetypes of brother and sister, balance and observation are required.

When one can observe a mate, who perhaps requires a motherly love, or brotherly advice, then it is up to the individual to rearrange themselves to allow them to rest with each other harmoniously. Like the elements, there is a constant ebb and flow differentially to maintain equilibrium. This requires deep and conscious restoration within.

Soul complexities can be enhanced via continual rebalancing, harmonising and recalibration of the subtle energies of the elements within the body. Many scriptures have been written on this but, with the simple primal images that have been mentioned previously, this can be a good place to start and effective for any being. Obviously, it is always good to keep being in a state of divine neutrality, so adaptation is easier. If we as individuals rest in a place of divine neutrality, we can in all relationships quickly adapt to have the skills we need to be of service within relationships to provide serenity, understanding and compassionate energies- as the service in essence is for one's own self to liberate and enlighten one's own journey.

GUIDANCE 4

Relinquishing all labels of who one's self is, is the key to unlocking the way of your own beauty. When one says, 'I am a ... ?' 'I am this or that', they are beholden to that very narrow label of a construct form, a society or collective. To be truly in spirit is to unnamed oneself, to be nothing- to be no- thing, to be everything in oneness. Broken spiritual ego will fight true oneness until it is exhausted by, and with, its means and only then can the individual, who has been held captive by the devices, regain consciousness. The individual will become and fulfil their destiny into their own unique spiritual self. Destiny is really just a plan you gave your soul, from spirit, before physical birth to keep oneself occupied. However, being in love and being love is paramount to any pre-ordained individual's destiny. Manifesting destiny is the way to love but if one is in love destiny is of no consequence as it will come to pass.

GUIDANCE 5

Beauty comes from truly believing you are divine.
Love holds no boundaries and dares all that embrace her.

Poem to Oshun
Honey and roses,
Rivers and forest,
Sun and moon,
Man and woman,
Love and life,
Child and innocence,
Green and pink,
Beauty and divinity,
Can never separate.
The Divine and the soul,
The Divine and the soul,
The Divine and the soul.

GUIDANCE 6

Love transcends all the notions of time it brings us into harmonic vibration that can only be felt from inside ones being that being said the radiation of this state causes everything around oneself to rearrange itself.

A deliberate clearing can come about when vibrations are realigned as the universe then provides the matches that harmonise with your own frequency.

Water is the planet and we are the water beings, if we can all vibrate to the essence of pure love the state of the planet, our mother water earth will be in complete harmony as will all nature and all beings.

At this time on mother water there are occurrences in effect to disharmonize the waters .We must not be dismayed as with a pure lake when a stone is thrown in eventually the lake levels and returns to calm water.

This is why sound is so very important and words today really bring mother water back to her equilibrium state as sound affects all of us and penetrates water to either be discordant or in-tune.

Nothing new is being said here as with all ancient traditions and cultures sound and music has always been integral in the divine humble existence on earth.

GUIDANCE 7

Sexuality , primality and sensuality.

Three profound energies and aspects to integrate into life consciously in union and harmony balance is vital.

Peace comes to those who fast, fast from all material distractions of the heart so the true mind, higher self remains.

Pure pure as the in-twinned DNA that rises from our spines like two snakes of vitality primal earth energy otherwise known as Shakti.

This energy is the primal base energy of being but it is misconstrued to be sexual energy.

Which it is too but requires to be harnessed instead of how it is wasted in many copulations. Thus the vitality and chi, life force energy of the person can be diminished.

Human beings must know how to use this vital force for pure love for union to be accomplished.

GUIDANCE 8

The nature of Human supreme being.

The realm of the formless in simple terms.

True nature is heart pure combined with absolute clear no mind. Some teachings only refer to the heart energy being enough however the higher mind the Ori (Yoruba word for higher self) determines your actions when ego mind is at bay thus if purified the heart can function effortlessly.

Heart energy is not enough if the higher mind gets taken away by egoic tendencies then it will go into temporal emotional states instead of spiritual enlightenment.

Thus it is cultivation of the mind and continuing opening of the heart that is acquired for ascension whilst physically in the body.

LOVE never dies but the key is to purify and wash the mind so that it too can transcend with the love in life and in re-incarnation.

If we can think in terms of **ONE MIND ONE HEART** this then becomes more apparent in the journey of enlightenment here and beyond the physical realm.

The human race has become somewhat focussed on the egoic mind and emotional heart like driving a car without petrol or not using the lights at night or even the steering wheel!

When Krishna takes control of Arjuna's chariot as he goes to battle, Krishna takes the reins of the horses (Arjuna's senses)so that he may overcome himself and rest in pure love whilst doing the work as a warrior he was sent to do on the earthly plane.

Overriding the egoic mind and emotional heart by surrendering completely to the universe the divine we all of us can truly BE supreme beings of GOLDEN LOVE LIGHT that we already ARE!

HEART ENERGY must be used alongside a clear 'Ori' mind for the greatest work on mother earth.

GUIDANCE 9

Today could be a day of infinite wisdom,

Infinite blessings,

There is nothing more blessed than being in the light.

The power of giving thanks and praise is phenomenal beyond the wildest thoughts of existence.

The nature of giving thanks and praise continues throughout space and time.

You can carry gratitude for eternity.

Give thanks and praise for yourself, for others, for nature, for matter, for mother earth, the SPIRIT-the universe.

GIVE THANKS AND PRAISE EVERYDAY FOR HUMBLENESS AND RIGHT ACTION AND TRUE FAIRNESS.

GUIDANCE 10

Yemoja-the sea feminine
Peace come like a wave from Yemoja,
Embrace you wash away your pain with one wave.
Straight away-ALL GONE-NO MORE discomfort.
Salt water from your inside out, spiritual salt water through ritual.

Way of Yemoja-continuous virtue you must cultivate amongst your peers.
Humbleness and pure love overcome ALL obstacles.

GUIDANCE 11

Regarding life cycles re-incarnation and the factors behind soul thoughts and remembrance of consciousness.

Trusting the brotherhood and sisterhood of Humankind-KIND-to live a dutiful kind life inducing the right step of action.

The right path followed-re-incarnation effortlessly, but if one boasts of incarnations in life go back to the start and erase all spiritual attributes acquired.

The lesson even when you know the way to remain conscious throughout your lives it is never a boastful subject and cannot be taught.

Obviously the more soul gardening in waking life of the physical the best prepared one is.

Spiritual adepts don't even see incarnation as challenging nor do they pre-occupy their time with it.

GUIDANCE 12

Forgiveness of the self

Humble way

Softness of being

Forgiving the masculine within and without.

Forgiving the feminine within and without.

Ultimately spirit is genderless but our incarnation leads us to take a man's form or a woman's form.

Essentially the aim is to unite the masculine principles with the feminine principles within each of us regardless of physical gender therein lies the lesson.

There was never any need to argue it was always the divine plan to just give each other pleasure and sacred union of two forms which were ultimately one before physical creation.

Relationship is deep respect and deep nurturing for each other if this ceases to exist the balance goes awry.

Growing up!!is the key to taking responsibilities and having adequate discipline and boundaries.

Devotion to oneself then another but firstly the divine which is us incarnate.

So being devoted to the self as an instrument of the divine is the way.

To be in the Christ-Cristos-crystalline light emerged from within ...

'Om Mani Padme Hum' the beautiful Tibetan mantra meaning' Hail to the jewel in the lotus',

The essence of the spirit within being the diamond of the heart the divine true nature purity love.

To be graceful in ways of navigation of the senses in all things.

Like Krishna and Arjuna in the Bhagavad Gita when Arjuna asks Krishna to take hold of the reins of his wild horses(his senses)of his chariot so that he can go into the world into the battle of the light that he has to win that his senses will be guided by his Krishna ,his higher self Cristos light.

Let the light take control of being in the right relationship with the self primarily then all of life because we are all and nothing surrender surrender surrender!!!

GUIDANCE 13

When the supremeness of light radiates through every cell of the body,

The joy and bliss that it permeates encompasses all that is love.'

In essence ... it is the essence of the divine we are from inside to outside.

Lifetimes we can keep adding to the shadow and shade ourselves from the light-the light-the truth now for all beings on MOTHER EARTH to come out from beneath the stone and bathe from inside the light of true being ,true oneness and follow —the way of beauty.

GUIDANCE 14

Ancestral reverence

If time doesn't exist then the pressure to do things is released; this does not stop the action but does give relief.

As TIME is the anomaly of fear of ultimately death of the flesh but the spirit is eternal so the construct of time is a device to aid the beings on the planet.

Ancestral time used to be with the cyclical nature of Mother Earth; modern man has literally gone against nature's own rhythm.

Thus the hearts of some men and women are not syncopated with the home which is the earth therefore there is massive discourse or dissonance of being.

Our timing is out !As a musician would say if one of the band was out of the time signature the whole piece of music falls apart.

The changes of the universe and mother earth are flowing with their own rhythm and cosmic law of order .Humans are the only form on the planet that are going against this divine order which is also the scientific law of cosmology and quantum physics.

It is then no surprise that humanity is suffering beyond all that was once thought.

The ridiculous notion that humans can destroy this planet is like saying a baby can lift a bull!

The only consequence of us as humans going out of heart rhythm is extinction of our race completely until creation starts again.

Any practice towards the light of being is required now.

All hearts must come into synchronisation to stabilise the energy of Mother Earth.

There are so many ways to do this, some are on the frontline, some are in the bush.

Staying positive and light is the key to the ascension of the rise of divine feminine and divine masculine to get the balance of the macro and micro in tune meaning the big and the small pictures in tune within ourselves and without into the world.

GUIDANCE 15

Sacred heart

Sacred light

Sacred waters

Are just three things to meditate upon to create heaven on earth.

All Solfeggio tones within music at this time will aid the recalibration of the planet (Mbira heavy dub reggae Bob Marley African ancient rhythms ragas classical Indian music basically any music from the people on the earth that still follow the ways of nature.

All music of grace, beauty and truth will uplift the planet.

Light codes from the sun help to recalibrate the DNA-ie sunbathing is essential.

So hold the light smile and remain good and honest at all times.

GUIDANCE 16

Self mastery-the coordinates for the way of beauty.

Patience-in all things

Love-with no condition

Tranquillity-of thoughts in the breath

Uprising-amidst adversity with gentleness

Collaboration-of mind ,spirit, soul ,heart inside beyond ether

Genuine-kindness character of being

Peace-continued across waterfall to river to sea

Interest-in losing yourself to the divine presence

Coordination-of the senses reigns supreme joy

GUIDANCE 17

The dissolution of the senses arises when love enters the heart in the purest free flowing form of true radiance like a flower that blooms its first essence is alight with a luminous hew of divinity in motion.

Unification of source via the heart can only be recognised when the higher self is at the forefront of the intellectual mind; the intellect is behind the heart secondary to love as essence.

One does not know any of this in one's mind, feel it as a tingling sensation through the spine … truth comes from such a depth that it is like a great whale rising from the ocean magnificence and awesome in the real sense that all pretence and masquerading is dissolved in an instance.

Be in this aquatic realm of sheer joy to eradicate suffering from the soul so the spirit can fly and feel its eternal grace of light in manifest flesh.

Peace is the illusion; this is the natural state after which refinement aligns to the vibration of what has always been within and without … benevolence.

Request nothing to surrender to all that is.

GUIDANCE 18

Everything in the mind is illusory
All that is true resides in the heart.

GUIDANCE 19

Divine feminine speaks ...
Stay neutral
Relinquish all that is needed.
Flow with your flow
Look after yourself
Put yourself first,
You are the gold.
Rare ,brilliant you are shining like a river in the sun.
You are honey from the bees.
Oshun in nature
She is beauty
Stay beautiful
Becoming more and more
Beautiful by loving yourself
So much and engaging with your divine masculine
That you are also complete within yourself.
You are wholy holy
You are magnificent
True honour from all around
When oneself honours their highest nature.
Shine shine shine your light!!!
Love overcomes all ...

GUIDANCE 20

This earth is cleansing herself. This is the agreement between Christ the sun and Sophia Gaia the earth.

To bring her light and cleanse and purify in rainbow light.

The rainbow light of the divine is beyond any light I have ever seen here on earth. The formless realm was so bright rainbow iridescent and so beautiful!

The same as earth but is more like a crystal rainbow like moonstone like a bozza ghost marble.

Thus this is the transformation to the new earth of rainbow crystalline light wow!

Solid light earth is very dense right now she is shrugging herself to crystallise.

Never ending bliss of rainbow iridescent light but like solid the formless realm it's engulfing its beyond bliss.

It never ends or begins; it is neither created nor death it just is!

That is what earth is aiming to become but in light frequency form.

Sparkly skin like diamond eyes and bodies will be iridescent but still in form with colour.

It will be a planet full of rainbow light but like a tiger will still have its distinct colours but glistening.

There will be no violence there will be no hunger, there will be no misuse of energies.

Gaia will return to being Solaris again a star and a rainbow Merkaba of spherical light will be her.

With a new name it will take quite a few more years and lifetimes 300 years

New children that are being conceived now will be rainbow light crystalline DNA.

GUIDANCE 21

Glimpse
Gracious timing and remembrance
That's all that's all
I could not think I could not breathe without you ...
The lesson to stand on my own magnitude.
By this I mean that I am divine
Because that is from whence I came ...
Oh how to love
How to give praise
How to give thanks
Oh how to say these words.

GUIDANCE 22

Release me from this dream
This dream which remains unseen
Release us from within
From within so we can be free
Peace from the core restore
Peace from the core re store
Re-align the love inside the shell
Re-define the unholy remembrance of denial

Flow aside flow inside with no pride
Do not hide around me ...
And do not hesitate to astound me..
Gently with ease and without disease
With ease.

GUIDANCE 23

Guidance on Relationships.

*use kindness to co-operate and heal

*do not be afraid of True Friendship

*acceptance of others flaws is vital

*non-distraction of your own core enables one to always BE present with relationship so one does not lose oneself becoming drained or swayed!

*absolute compassion

(Reminder of this my Grandmothers making time yet having boundaries even in her presence-loving ALL including the tiny sparrow birds.

Equally crying for someone yet not being attached to the tears from them or yourself).

*TRUST -if one has solid trust in the universe this is part of being the great oneness.

Oneness of being-TRUST is natural trust is the cosmic self the essence of divine within pure spirit.

The soul being part of the whole one must trust in the spirit to clean the soul to be immersed in everlasting eternal grace of the divinity of the oneness of being formlessly radiant within love.

If people or situations are detrimental when the core is still nothing can bend it!

Along with this notion a sense of when to engage and to disengage is essential one does not have to cut off.

Remain in one's core aligned with the divine AT ALL TIMES.

THERE IS NO OTHER PLACE TO BE!

GUIDANCE 24

Glimpse
Rivers the veins
Waters the blood
Like our bodies
The same on Mother Earth
This is the greater understanding of true being.
The micro and the macro of all life.

GUIDANCE 25

The word of love is destroyed if there is negative speech.

Pristine words cool and temper an angered soul like a sweet summer breeze and a droplet of sparkling water from an ocean.

Regain your self sovereignty by not engaging in the sounds of a language that does not ring the celestial tone of grace and of beauty.

That being said, may all the flowers of the earth, stars of the sky and waters of the rivers of the oceans waterfall on your sacred being and cleanse every part of you so that the feeling of transient love remains as warmth in the tender fire of your heart.

Droplets of light rainbows of angelic wisdom sturdy grace of the lion spirit ancestors enrapture all that you are.

Never doubt the essence of the divine within you.

Grace in character

Beauty in action

Sweet waters ... calm sounds ...

GUIDANCE 26

The union of hearts has many twists and turns whilst it plays out the dance to reunite a harmonious oneness.

The heart fire of the masculine and the heart fire of the feminine must unite within yourself primarily by this balance within is accomplished.

This is the water and fire, the moon and sun, the yin and yang ,the darkness and the light in colours red and blue.

Only when this balance occurs can the celestial fire of two beings unite.

However relationships do enable this to occur so must not be avoided even if the union within has not yet finally been attained.

Relationships serve human BEINGS to go into the practical ways of processing oneself to clean up the soul and function from true spirit.

Spirit is never unclean or clean —spirit is the pulsation of the divine life force that keeps ALL things alive in the universe.

We must never worry that we can lose spirit. It is the souls which we have chosen to work on and refine that is the main concern here.

Souls like homes need cleaning so we have two jobs keeping the soul clean and the physical body yet if both are surrendered and guided by pure spirit in turn pure mind pure heart destiny is made manifest.

Returning again to the heart fire and union of masculine and feminine, our duty individually is to keep maintaining the fire path just like a normal physical fire so it does not go out.

Concerning union in the physical especially with twin flames this is vital as when the two flames come together as one it is usually spiritually first and then the emotions and physical can take longer hence separation and loss. Heart pains can be felt this is an indicator to keep stoking the fire.

The construct society of perpetual navigation to cause separation to be on one's own.

Individuality- self ,self ,self makes the female and male union especially challenging. It is like the moon and sun warring at each other ,yet in true nature one needs the other and both are always present in mother earth's field.

As progression on this planet to a more conscious way of life we must consider these gifts from the divine to remind us we are not alone and that being together is a natural way of beauty.

Never give up on the sacred heart in its power and ability to burn through any pains or discomforts.

The fire from the heart is celestial primordial ALL powerful. The energy of love can purify the darkest of corners and penetrate the confused minds of humanity.

Challenges will always come but if the fire is burning the soul is warm and nothing can freeze it.

Ignite the flames of masculine and feminine within, dance together and shine bright from your heart and smile from your inside glow.

Love is the birth of life!

GUIDANCE 27

To incarnate on earth was to merely experience being in a physical reality with feelings and senses in relation to the other.

Relationship!

Spirit coming into form but not being lost in form.

We are not form, we are formless incarnated into form.

It is something like being attached to the walls of your house as if they are part of you.

The body is just the house and the senses the furniture enjoy but always know that you are of no form —stillness.

GUIDANCE 28

From divine feminine

The Aspect called Oshun.

To feel absolute luscious beauty from within and without.

To bathe the heart in the sweet waters of kindness, softness and divine strength flow sacred rivers as honey does to the bees.

Drink the nectar of life in ...

Moisturise the heart with all the radiance of the diamond light of the solaris star

Golden we are .. rose tinted light

Enraptures the soul ... grace in action.

GUIDANCE 29

The Rose line the Heart chakra and rebalancing to live in LOVE.

Whether or not you choose love

For yourself or another

Embracing the truth about yourself at all times is paramount.

In doctrine in the system of the west is constant separation and collaged feelings of disenfranchisement of the sexes.

Meaning male and female at unease with each other via manipulation.

The remedy is to constantly balance the energies from within to increase harmony from without.

GUIDANCE 30

To the divine light within

Aiding oneself to still the senses of the mind.

Relax the body, the spirit rests and the whole being can become calm waters..sweet sounds.

The harmony, the peace within where the love in the heart resides.

Igniting the heart fire but keeping the coolness of sweet water is to bring male and female energy within us into balance.

Thus a more virile nature and soft way of being can ensue.

Nurture the softness and radiance of the heart in essence being of love as the biggest greatness not a weakness.

GUIDANCE 31

Remedy

Practising grounding being here now..

Feet firmly planted on the earth and spine long with head connected to the sky it is our purpose to experience a physical reality in the amazing instrument the body whilst we reside in our hotel as a guest planet earth.

Therefore either being too earthbound or too sky bound will not work watching the sun constantly sparkling in the sky shining down to create movement of the waves of the ocean inspires me to recognise the absolute vital need to being here in presence that we are made of the elements-earth wind fire water and Akash(ether).

That we are also spirits inside the temple experiencing senses of touch sight hearing taste and smell.

We are beyond the senses and are magnificent beings of experiential capabilities but to get lost in the 'Siddhis' as Patangalis Yoga sutras state is to miss the point of being in a physical vessel.

Nonetheless to get trapped in just the physical is also a waste of life thus the two need to combine in a healthy manner.

This can take so much time and extensive learning or it can be instant some say just by sitting and closing the eyes the kingdom is within the universe the divine there resides.

I personally overstand that every being on this planet is unique and has their own journey that every being ultimately is seeking real love-not emotional but formless-unconditional love which inherently was where we all came from.

We are each of us divine sparks of the whole cosmos experiencing our own uniqueness our own journeys yet we are one this is the way to hold each other not grasp but like a butterfly on the palm of a hand exist together respecting and honouring each beings beauty experience benevolence and mystery as normal.

Respect comes with boundaries and acceptance of another yet hurting another is not the way and with diligent communication humanity can reach this position of totality of being in togetherness unity consciousness.

GUIDANCE 32

Trees
Sturdy roots bend with the wind
But always rooted firm in Mother earth-
Magnificent pure being togetherness
In truth
Grounded stay flexible but grounded.

GUIDANCE 33

Divine feminine

Love holds no boundaries

Peace child peace

Abundance to you in every way

Do not dissipate what you are to receive

Stay strong and steadfast in all your dealings.

Do not be fooled by the humbleness of being this is a gift not a burden.

Always love unconditionally

Do not waiver your heart for any lover

Keep misused feminine tendencies art bay.

Never hold onto anything or anyone

Be present —SING -LOVE

GUIDANCE 34

From that which cannot see, let all worries of love be taken away.

Meaning if the chosen person cannot see the love in the other soul then they must cultivate love from within their sacred temple and wash away the cloudiness that only serves as a veil to their own exuberance and diamond like clarity of perfect being that they are.

Once the maya or illusion from within is washed away then all the beauty in everything upon the earth is seen as it is.

Miracles become normality and love is standard giving, receiving is in equal measure and polarity of male and female sun and sea is rested upon like a feather in a cool breeze effortlessly and in balance nothing is pulling or pushing simple ebb and flow of divinity within and without.

The sun shines always on the waters illuminating their glory and the waters reflect back the magnificence of the star our sun.

GUIDANCE 35

Reason needs no discovery
　　When the heart is bathed
　　In the fires of purity.

Love holds no-one in control nor does it let you go with no holding for true love is eternally safe and warm as the heart beats inside the Mothers body the infant hears the primal call and is known that the unknown is all around.

Inside the womb is dark we are blind and in water we are pure in creation, primal waters being in being created. How strange that once released into the light we are then afraid of the dark of the unknown of creation from which we came.

GUIDANCE 36

Love over all conquers all,

    For it is impermeable and unrelinquishable,

    In its adept way to protect and heal the heaviest of hearts.

    Primary function of challenges in life on all levels is to enrich ourselves to the highest state to become all one with love inside and out.

    To radiate harmonic frequencies that are palpable to uplift the notion of freedom in context with living in a constrict constructive society so far removed from the higher angelic realms and to earth spiritual ancestral realms that it is vital to connect with both therefore bringing heaven together with earth in remembrance of reverence .

    True beauty knows no boundaries.

    True beauty blossoms in the heart of all sentient beings.

    True nurturing is paramount to divinity in action.

GUIDANCE 37

Be who you are!

By not being who you are meaning eternal stillness that pervades all terror fear and anxiety

Into the ocean of the sanctuary

That is the heart of all purpose

That is light of the whole universe-the illumined soul

Collective spirit

Collective love . . .

GUIDANCE 38

Perception

Realising that every person perceives their own reality from the inside their being is key to acceptance, forgiveness and comparison ultimately to enlightenment.

I like to think of colours as a child. I always thought of why red was red and why green was green etc! Was my sister seeing the same colours as me?

The truth is we will never know what science can try to explain but I think it's only if one can see from another's eyes which is impossible.

Maybe this is the teaching to always metaphysically see from another's perspective and perception in a neutral and non-emotional manner.

Herein lies the challenge within the intimacy of some relationships, especially romantic in nature. True perception can become mired by the maya.

The whole illusion of one's sense perception in essence the more we clean ourselves from the inside out the clearer we can see and relate in true fusion accordingly with humanity honesty grace and integrity above all with no judgement.

Rational sane mind that vibrates from the heart of true love that is neutral in tone is perhaps the resonance that humanity needs to start perceiving from and embracing for a healthier relationship and ultimately a peaceful and vibrantly filled unity existence on earth.

GUIDANCE 39

Relationships –romantic

Perception of the male and female dynamics.

Divine lessons to release all preconceptions of what women or men should or shouldn't be so we can see beyond gender the physical possessing the attributes simply going with the heart.

This takes work a dissolving of the matrix of pleasures and trusting in the universe.

If one does not move or work to relieve unhappy situation in relationship karma the universal law will do it for you as to the universe time does not exist so the choice is yours no matter what or when the karma is played out regardless of time one realises and is truly humbled to the fact that one was never in control!!!

We are here to learn and learn. We will do it the easy way or the hard way.

In essence it comes down to letting go and surrendering to the truth of your heart ,dissolving the illusions the constructs and trusting in the divine true universe-the unknown.

Look at the stars. They are in perfect order. The universe has its order and who are we to think we know better than it?

Imagine if every being looked at the stars at the same time on earth stopped for a breath ,breathed together realising the oneness and totality of us all the magnificence and awe …

GUIDANCE 40

Christ consciousness revelations-starlight

To love yourself as you love the Christ

To love your beloved as you love the Christ

Love yourself as much as you love Jeshua

Love your man as if he is the Christ

Submit to his love —not his will

Release the warrior aspect and embrace the soft way of feminine power-
the beauty-the grace-the ease..

No more protecting of others —spiritual ego just be

Be love —beloved

Christ —Christ consciousness truth-Cristos diamond way of truth.

GUIDANCE 41

Sacred fire and cooling waters

    Unifying to immerse the soul

    Into perfection of depth of sequential love.

    Hold not your heart in captivity but nurture it with gentleness and grace of antiquity.

    Cool your mind Trust your spirit!

GUIDANCE 42

Female and male dynamic

The female's ever changing flow of elemental water ebb and rise/flow like the moon waxing and waning ,the male straight in form precise direct sparkling iridescent soul/soul single pointed –burning.

How then do we unite those within ourselves and then somehow unite eternally?

Essentially the teachings of love are wrong in these times of modernity'

Romantic love is not real

Real love is not romantic

The heart sighs of so many but what is real is far greater than romance...

It is just in our conditioning that we have come to believe love is overstated, exciting, demanding without emotional boundaries ;this is transient and becomes a trapped place as one realises after a while this is not sustainable.

Real love is quiet, soft, emotionally contained, understated, calm no expectations no conditions for this is true love and freedom yet strangely this reality takes massive constraint and work of one's senses that want to run riot.

Thus the constant interchange of female and male characteristics within oneself is challenging enough so to recognise one's differences states is key thus one can recognise the others state read it and know how to engage .Neutrality is a gift to all as sometimes it can be extremely hard to navigate a relationship not only with oneself but then with another simultaneously.

What leads to disharmony is lack of AWARENESS of first how the individual feels to then consideration of the other.

All relationships on this planet are about awareness and therefore the lack of it causes a disharmony in the balance of humanity.

Imagine a world where all relationships were based on considerate awareness of the self in relation to the other. How do they feel? How can we create harmony inside and outside?

Fundamentally this is the only reason we are here on this our mother the earth.

To be nurtured and to nurture

To be natural and in nature

To be love and beloved

GUIDANCE 43

Love unconditional
Is divine acceptance of each other as they are..
No wanting or needing this is illusory!

The emotion of love is so powerful it can lead oneself to ultimate bliss and excruciable pain therefore it is transient and only peace from the innocence of true love divine light from within will EVER bring constant equilibrium.

However there is no drama here and thus the ego will endeavour to find some way of causing some the key is to maintain the inside self sovereignty Krishna Christ light from within Vajrasattva the diamond way of cutting through the maya and illusion to not be swayed by the tricks and games of the ego the shadow self.

Always remove oneself if in the middle of such drama if not physically, spiritually and energetically.

Decide which role you want to play in the game of life.

GUIDANCE 44

Patience is acquiescence in your state of being for one to really know another is to regulate one's behaviour primarily before engaging with another.

A humble detached approach is required to debilitate any sort of re-action.

Action and rest these are the two primal principles of engagement that arise from the formless realm the divine the Tao , Ifa (unknown formless)

No compromise in any way this is also tangible and interchangeable throughout time even down to the second thus extra diligence is always required in interaction with another being.

GUIDANCE 45

The nature of phenomena.

In the physical world all things arise consequently from a desire from the mind thus most actions are derived from one's ego unless the mind-Ori is washed clean then the actions arise from the Tao Ifa a water like state of being of diamond purity in order to be within the divine code of being.

Ultimately a warrior of light engaged in dismantling the shadow of the suppressive world ego is only attained by being present nothing more nothing less.

GUIDANCE 46

Divinity through action
Grace through steady perseverance
Beauty from inside being
Sanctity through nurture.

GUIDANCE 47

Self mastery -co-ordinates for living in the way of beauty.

Patience-in all things

Love-without condition

Tranquillity-of thoughts in the breath

Uprising-amidst adversity with gentleness

Collaboration -of mind spirit soul heart inside beyond any other concern.

Genuine –kindness

Peace- continued from across the waterfall to the river to the sea meaning still water in different forms.

Interest-in losing oneself to the divine

Coordination of the senses reigns supreme joy

GUIDANCE 48

Celestial fire pure sweet waters to balance eternal flame.

Celestial flame of grace of heaven enraptured the spirit living on earth as the cool waters kept the spirit cool and vibrant.

This is not in elemental terms this is in spiritual nonlinear terms it is a metaphor for peaceful living.

Too little fire or too little water or too much fire and too much water are off balance equal flame to cool water is required for spiritual enlightenment thus being at one with the only truth which is the oneself there is only one self!

GUIDANCE 49

Huge changes are afoot on celestial mother earth,

Creation as the human race is ever changing and evolving thus notions of greatness must be dispelled for all to rise with and in love.

It is for all to BE in LOVE not just separation in couples.

In conclusion, embrace all that flows like oceans of time, the rivers of antiquity, the grace of paradise, the love of truly being the summer of the heart is all that humanity can live equally in to enfold peace and truth and live an honest existence.

GUIDANCE 50

The realm of choice is combined with the realm of possibility.

Uniting spirit and flesh to be absolute human beings.

Uniting Masculine and feminine, heaven and earth.

Spirit sees white roses flesh expressed in red roses.

The main purpose and delight of this book is how to unite the two to become truly celestial beings on physical earth.

Remedy

Rose way of light-Using divination through nature

Using petals for medicine -rose oil essential for ingestion to calm the heart(only a drop in a glass of water and test on skin before for allergy never ingest neat essential oil).

Words of relaxation

Relax your senses

Body relax-relax into your physical body

Spirit relax into your body

Patience …

Calm still waters

No hurry no rush … stop trying.

GUIDANCE 51

Receive everything with grace and ease, humility and kindness.

See everything and everybody as gentle petals in the sweet spring breeze.

Grace with ease-soft overcomes the hard.

Softening of our hearts to live in a gentle way for all male and female incarnates.

All that is true remains in the heart; there is no other truth to this grace of life.

One can either surrender to it or fight it one causes eternal joy the other obviously does not.

GUIDANCE 52

Inspirations from Oshun.

A manuscript for living daily embracing all that is beautiful in the truly mundane existence; searching not to the stars but within to discover the moving cosmos each radiant spirit wrapped in the cloths of heaven are; meaning every human being every animal ,bird ,aquatic life form is that on mother earth.

Simple gestures of love to the self and others in a daily mundane existence is the meaning of enlightenment it is vibrant and so subtle-classic saying of stop to smell the roses is exactly enlightenment in its entirety, as simplicity of beauty awakens each and every soul to realise they are ever eternal spirit of purity and wholly holy!

LOVE never masquerades or defeats a soul only ignites each divine spark of source realisation.

CRAVING another never leads to peace only greed and jealousy; therefore relinquish all notion that one human owns another in all relationship parents ,lover ,brother ,sister !Release each and all by true oneness of unconditional Love for another no attachment no remorse only tolerance and patience.

Never underestimate one's ego in the conquest to herald pure love vibration meaning when the heart is pure the mind must also be too so the two can work in tandem and no arresting notion of negative thought can sabotage the diamond state of living as one in the way of beauty.

Always listen to the beauty within your sensuous soul your eternal spirit which reigns down all the love from THE DIVINE onto yourself cleansing and washed as in a river this is she this is we for all is clandestine in nature all is soft sweet scents of rainbow light all are flowers within flowers ,sun within sun moon within moon light within dark dark within light ,ever changing ever eternal always remaining the same from creation divine sparks divine sparks.

It is for ALL to BE in LOVE not just separation of couple s creation as the human race is ever changing and evolving notions of individual greatness must be dispelled for all to rise with and in LOVE.

Embrace all that flows like the oceans of time ,the rivers of antiquity ,the grace of paradise ,the love of truly being ,the summer of the heart is all that humanity can live in equally to enfold peace-truth and honest existence.

Heaven the fire;
Earth the water;
Form the diamond truth.
Celestial fire pure sweet waters embrace to balance eternal flame.
The celestial flame of grace of heaven enraptured in the spirit,
Living on earth as the cool waters.

To keep the spirit cool and vibrant- not in elemental terms this is
In spiritual non literal/linear terms a metaphor for peaceful living;
Too little fire too much water,
Too much fire too little water,
Equal flame to equal cool water,
Equals spiritual enlightenment.

GUIDANCE 53

Oshun reminders of self preservation.

Never determine your standards by another's

*Keep to your internal rhythm

*UPHOLD your senses and do not let them be led by perception of outside influences

*BREATHE...

*BE gentle and kind in character -do not give rise to tacless words and unnecessary speaking.

*Be bold and brave-courageousness does not require brute strength-only the flow and current of active waters —River river river...

*Acquire good nature from the Elders —the teachings of Ancestor

*Be good ...

*Be kind to yourself; if you have been harsh —correct it with inside meditation forgiveness and learning to not do it AGAIN!!!

*Repetition of unnatural tendencies-egoic states only leads to one's demise-ie not preservation —degradation of the soul —not living via IPONR(highest

self in Yoruba)I by negating pure being by cloudy ,musty ,being-HONOUR YOUR ORI!!!

*Create heaven on earth-in all your dealings no matter how big or small.

*Rescue yourself from negative thoughts that only lead to self-masochistic behaviour

*Control your sexual urges when not appropriate in timing and space context —self control- self control- self control

*Do not hold blame or have it anywhere in your being —it is a powerful potent destructive emotion to cease all enlightenment paths

*Anger has no place in the heart

*Fear does not reside in true nature

*Discrimination of any kind is cowardice in motion-end this race

*Above all LOVE BE LOVE ... BE LOVED ... BE-ING LOVE ...

GUIDANCE 54

The Time of Grace.

The moment between inhale and exhale —it exists yet it does not —the child before it becomes a gender-pure soul yet in form-fragile creation stage, but the soul is already there so remembering this is paramount in connection with true self in form yet genderless-NO IDENTITY.

IDENTITY is ego therefore to witness creation is to connect with a non-egoic state of being.

Using the cycles of life:

Moon/Luna

Sun/Solar

Plants

Sea etc . . .

The menstrual cycle is a celebration of creation and shedding of form and formlessness of potential life every month —this is powerful and a woman's birthright to experience it!

As with all the cyclical systems of nature-we are not linear and as we continue to live in a binary linear fashion loss of the womb of the divine and the divine seasonal is being lost.

Hence human beings get ill when not adhering to seasonal beings.

Men's Luna cycle is practically lost in the west. When it is realised that everything is alive it gives meaning to LIFE on this planet so much more than one can imagine.

65

Meditate -extreme gravitas to this latter statement for humankind to truly resonate with for eternity ...

GUIDANCE 55

Beauty transcends all that appears to be dark, allowing light to harness itself to unite and bring joy and peace.

Configuration and divine protection is always available to the kind in heart.

Blessings come to those who earn them and this is not about money or a job.

This is about conciliation of the soul of clarity of a supposed dream-that is and has never been REAL.

The Medicine of sweet waters is one that cannot be taught only experienced.

By ingesting sacred sweet waters of a river peace and clarity ensued sensual vision and extreme healing.

Intuition increased calming of the soul and calming equilibrium within the cells physically feeling like being in waves and, waves within

Waves inside calming waters within.

Tumours melted away

Cravings of the mind, simple pleasures inhabit real life force energy.

Oshun river water taken internally revealed destiny but slowly the gravitational pull of the waters will allow you to visit a place of absolute tranquillity and sacredness and clarity to feel God.

Attributes with meditations of the soul work.

Reasonable intellect

Clarified automated specific sight-removal of egoic shroud on each individual

Pacing one's actions

Unglorified attention to one's self (materially and physically)

Adaptability to surroundings with unshakable core

Diet requirements for specific work

Ie white fish-writing/manifesting/meditation

Sugar sweet food for planetary upheaval/shifts

Social awareness saying what only needs to be said and nothing more.

Quiet inside structures of time in conjunction with being able to function in the collective supra mundane world

Guided supervision from an elder-

As all senses develop and more is revealed the eternal self/spirit of the person must be checked on to make sure the person does not become de-ranged due to overload and overwhelming presence

Of being awake for the first time in adult life.

Humbleness again, again, again

Like the way of the TAO the way of water keeps your balance going up and down the ladder of the experience that is life and your feet on the ground.

See the world as yourself the outer mirrors the inner

In regard to this, be diligent in what you put your attention to. It is your choice.

Appropriation of the senses.

Subtle treatment to clarify —head ,fingertips ,heart ,feet

In love —with God and all that is

One must control the senses with great fortitude, temptations are everywhere and distraction imminent.

The truth will out

No one and nothing can hide

Cravings come and go but steadiness is paramount

Calming of the soul-spiritual grace between two beings is true love.

Unification with celestial light within on earth always stays grounded as protection.

Humbleness

Friendship

Elements of true friendship ,true love-recognising each other's beauty

-kindness

-humble

-radiant

-fairness

GUIDANCE 56

Glimpse

Journey of healing through absolute determination and faith in oneself and surrender to the divine.

If you take from mother earth and do not put anything back energy- for- energy!

You will never find the divine within.

True service is cyclical.

GUIDANCE 57

Embrace all that flows like the oceans of time, the rivers of antiquity ,the grace of paradise ,the love of truly being ,the summer of the heart is all that humanity can live equally in to enfold peace-truth and honest existence.

Creation as the human race is ever changing and evolving ,notions of who is the greatest must be dispelled for all to rise with and in love.

It is for all to BE in LOVE not just couples.

GUIDANCE 58

Clearing the obstacles of the emotional mind especially for women during hormonal cycles.

By using the masculine aspect we can cut through the emotional mire. This can balance the linear diamond cutting direct force within us by using the feminine aspect of nurturing and gentle soft way of doing things.

Both in extremity are out of balance so a constant play between the two aspects is the way to self mastery.

Male in union with female in the physical gives way to the male fire to warm and heat the female thus the female gives way to the male to cool and temper the heat-not burn or freeze.

A cool way of union like a summer breeze.

In brief, man heats woman, woman cools man.

Fire and water as the elements combining creates the celestial fire within the heart ignites the spirit.

It is therefore not about gender it is about the two aspects sun and moon fire and water Shiva and Shakti Auset and Osar bees and flowers.

The beauty in union is the male aspect igniting the heart fire and the female aspect cools and nourishes with the sweet waters and the nectar from the celestial fire.

GUIDANCE 59

That which comes from love has no longing or intellect,

The power of unity breaks into or over any constructed notion of identity of the I and only remains in the knowing of the self.

In the true form of togetherness that there is only ONESELF-ONE-SELF.

Harmony cannot exist without this wisdom and all who align to this with bravery and courage

Can take anything in the construct world of the egoic mind!

Therefore always come back to the core of being of reality that is truth that incarnate from the oceans to the wonder of the palms and the inside creation of the divinity held in ALL beings!

EPILOGUE

'The cloth is the earth
　　And we the jewels
　　sewn upon it'
　　White Buffalo Woman inspired

To be inspired that is all I search for like a butterfly flitting from flower to flower seeing the beauty of many varieties and experiencing new colours.

I Know there is more to come but for now if I had wished for all this then I would truly believe I was greedy but none of this did I wish for or even imagine but somehow happened for this I am truly blessed.

These dreams exist and are the 'clothes of heaven' for I have been swaddled in the finest, most wondrous and divinely beautiful fabrics that could have been made!